Totally Wacky
Roadside
Attractions

by Pamela Chanko

Content Consultant
Robbin Friedman, Children's Librarian
Chappaqua (N.Y.) Library

Reading Consultant
Jeanne M. Clidas, Ph.D.
Reading Specialist

Children's Press®
An Imprint of Scholastic Inc.

J
READER   *-33-5437*

Library of Congress Cataloging-in-Publication Data

Names: Chanko, Pamela, 1968- author.
Title: Totally wacky roadside attractions/by Pamela Chanko.
Description: New York, NY: Children's Press, an imprint of Scholastic Inc.,
2017. | Series: Rookie amazing America | "Produced by Spooky Cheetah Press." | Includes index.
Identifiers: LCCN 2016030334| ISBN 9780531228982 (library binding) | ISBN 9780531225929 (pbk.)
Subjects: LCSH: Roadside architecture—United States—Juvenile literature. |
Curiosities and wonders—United States—Juvenile literature. | Automobile
travel—United States—Juvenile literature.
Classification: LCC NA682.R63 C43 2017 | DDC 917.3—dc23
LC record available at https://lccn.loc.gov/2016030334

Produced by Spooky Cheetah Press

© 2017 by Scholastic Inc.

Printed in China 62

SCHOLASTIC, CHILDREN'S PRESS, ROOKIE AMAZING AMERICA™, and associated logos are trademarks
and/or registered trademarks of Scholastic Inc.

1 2 3 4 5 6 7 8 9 10 R 26 25 24 23 22 21 20 19 18 17

Photographs ©: cover: Glenn Nagel/Dreamstime; back cover main: Franck Fotos/Alamy Images;
back cover sky: ooyoo/iStockphoto; 3 sky: IP Galanternik D.U./iStockphoto; 3 main: Steve Lagreca/
Dreamstime; 4 main: Franck Fotos/Alamy Images; 4 sky: ooyoo/iStockphoto; 7: Andreykr/Dreamstime;
8 left: John Bazemore/AP Images; 8 bottom right: Bettmann/Getty Images; 9 main: Mike Theiss/Getty
Images; 9 inset: pixhook/iStockphoto; 11 main: Franck Fotos/Alamy Images; 11 sky: IP Galanternik D.U./
iStockphoto; 12-13: Steve Lagreca/Dreamstime; 14: Franck Fotos/Alamy Images; 15: RoadsideAmerica.
com; 16: LOOK Die Bildagentur der Fotografen GmbH/Alamy Images; 17 main: Glenn Nagel/
Dreamstime; 17 inset: Images-USA/Alamy Images; 18 main: Jordan McAlister/Getty Images; 18 inset:
PAINTING/Alamy Images; 19: Lee Foster/Alamy Images; 20: Rose-Marie Murray/Alamy Images; 21:
Jessica Bolin; 22-23 main: Michael Hurcomb/Getty Images; 23 top inset: Elizabeth W. Kearley/Getty
Images; 23 bottom inset: Education Images/Getty Images; 24: Inge Johnsson/Alamy Images; 26-27
background: 123ducu/iStockphoto; 26 top left: Franck Fotos/Alamy Images; 26 top center: Andreykr/
Dreamstime; 26 top right: John Bazemore/AP Images; 26 center top left: Mike Theiss/Getty Images;
26 center top: Franck Fotos/Alamy Images; 26 center top right: Steve Lagreca/Dreamstime; 26 center
bottom left: Franck Fotos/Alamy Images; 26 center bottom: Glenn Nagel/Dreamstime; 26 center
bottom right: Jordan McAlister/Getty Images; 26 bottom left: Jessica Bolin; 26 bottom center: Michael
Hurcomb/Getty Images; 26 bottom right: Inge Johnsson/Alamy Images; 28-29 background: ooyoo/
iStockphoto; 28 main: SiliconValleyStock/Alamy Images; 29 main: Tyler W. Stipp/Shutterstock, Inc.; 30
main: Franck Fotos/Alamy Images; 30 background: 123ducu/iStockphoto; 31 top: Jordan McAlister/
Getty Images; 31 center top: Franck Fotos/Alamy Images; 31 center bottom: Inge Johnsson/Alamy
Images; 31 bottom: Elizabeth W. Kearley/Getty Images; 32 main: Steve Lagreca/Dreamstime; 32 sky: IP
Galanternik D.U./iStockphoto.

Maps by Jim McMahon.

Table of Contents

Introduction

The Donut Hole,
La Puente, California

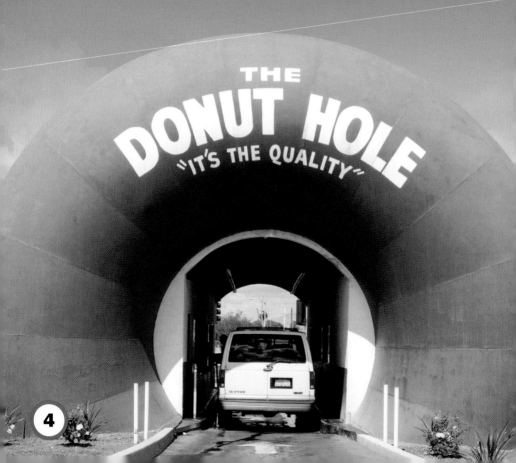

What is this giant donut doing in a parking lot? A donut shop is inside! You can buy donuts from your car. This big donut is a roadside attraction. That is a place along the side of the road that was made to attract people driving by.

There are lots of amazing roadside attractions across the United States. Let's explore some more!

Funny Food

Imagine the ice cream sundae you could eat with this spoon! It is actually a bridge.

A pair of married artists created the bridge. It is in a park in Minnesota. The husband liked to draw spoons. The cherry was the wife's idea. She thought it would make the park more fun.

Totally Wacky!

Water sprays out of the cherry's stem.

This big peanut was made to honor Jimmy Carter. He was our 39th president. Before that, he was a peanut farmer. The peanut is in his hometown. Does the peanut's smile look like the president's smile?

President Jimmy Carter

This is really nutty! It is the world's largest pistachio. It stands outside Pistachio Tree Ranch, a farm in New Mexico.

pistachio

World's Largest Pistachio, Alamogordo, New Mexico

Cool Creatures

Meet Lucy the Elephant. She is bigger than any real elephant. She is over six stories tall! You can even go inside. A staircase is in her leg.

Visitors can climb up and see a museum, which tells Lucy's story. She was built by the beach in New Jersey. Her owner wanted to get people interested in buying land nearby. Now Lucy is a **National Historic Landmark**.

**Lucy the Elephant,
Margate, New Jersey**

At one point, a family rented Lucy as a beach house! Inside, they built bedrooms, a kitchen, and a dining room. They even built a bathroom in her shoulder.

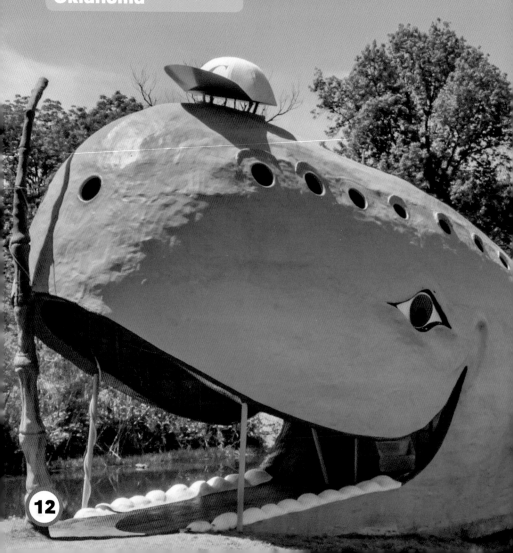

Ol' Blue, the Blue Whale of Catoosa, Oklahoma

Oklahoma is not near an ocean. But this big blue whale is right at home there. It sits in a pond. The whale's nickname is Ol' Blue. It was built by an animal scientist. It was a gift for his wife.

Today visitors can go inside the whale's mouth.

Queen Connie,
Leicester,
Vermont

This gorilla was built to help sell cars. But the car in its hand is not for sale. (Yes, that is a real car!)

The gorilla's other hand reaches down to the ground. Why? So people can climb up and sit in it, of course.

Totally Wacky!

Every giant gorilla needs a name, so a naming contest was held. The winner was "Queen Connie of Concrete." She has been called Queen Connie ever since.

Amazing Art

Imagine driving down a dusty road. Then you see 10 colorful cars sticking out of the ground! This is no traffic accident. It is Cadillac Ranch, and it is a work of art.

Cadillac Ranch was created by three artists. The row of cars is at the edge of a cow pasture.

Totally Wacky! Visitors are allowed to bring spray paint and make their mark. That is how the cars stay so colorful.

The original painting is called *Three Sunflowers in a Vase*. Do you think the artist did a good job copying it?

This huge copy of a Van Gogh painting is in Goodland, Kansas.

18

More than 125 years ago, a famous artist named Vincent van Gogh (VIN-sunt van GOH) made 11 paintings of sunflowers. Now another artist is making giant copies of the paintings. You can see them on huge **easels** around the world.

Vincent van Gogh

One of those big paintings is in Kansas. That is the perfect spot. Kansas is nicknamed the Sunflower State.

Larger Than Life

If you were a giant, where would you keep your clothes? The World's Largest Chest of Drawers is in High Point, North Carolina. The town is known for making furniture.

The clothes inside are huge, too! The socks are six feet tall, about the size of a grown man.

The World's Largest Chest of Drawers, High Point, North Carolina

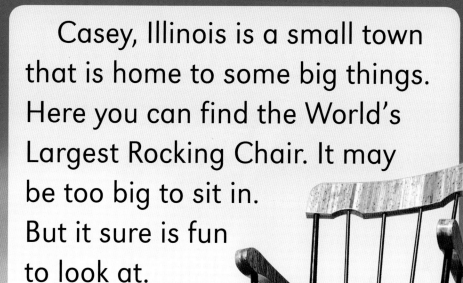

Casey, Illinois is a small town that is home to some big things. Here you can find the World's Largest Rocking Chair. It may be too big to sit in. But it sure is fun to look at.

World's Largest Rocking Chair, Casey, Illinois

Totally Wacky!

Other big things in Casey include the World's Largest Wind Chimes and the World's Largest Knitting Needles. The town would make a perfect home for the World's Largest Grandma!

Having a Ball

There are **water towers** all over our country. They are not usually fun to look at. But some towns have a ball with them! Can you name each type of ball on the water towers shown here?

Eye,
Dallas, Texas

If you visit Dallas, Texas, you might feel like you are being watched. After all, there is a giant eyeball sitting in town! The artist who created the **sculpture** made it to look like his own eyes. But this eye never blinks!

There are amazing roadside attractions all over America. Would you like to see some for yourself? Just keep your eyes open.

United States

Look at the number on each roadside attraction. Find it on the map.

1
The Donut Hole

2
Spoonbridge and Cherry

3
Jimmy Carter Peanut Statue

Washington

Montana

4
World's Largest Pistachio

5
Lucy the Elephant

6
Blue Whale of Catoosa

Oregon

Idaho

Nevada

Utah

California

7
Queen Connie

8
Cadillac Ranch

9
Giant Van Gogh Painting

1

Arizona

10
World's Largest Rocking Chair

11
Beach Ball Water Tower

12
Giant Eyeball Sculpture

Alaska

Hawaii

Alaska and Hawaii are not drawn to scale or placed in their proper places.

of America

New Hampshire
Michigan
Vermont   Maine
North Dakota   Minnesota
Massachusetts
2   Wisconsin
South Dakota   **7**
New York   Rhode Island
Connecticut
oming   Iowa   Pennsylvania   New Jersey
Nebraska   Ohio   **5**   Delaware
Illinois   Indiana   West Virginia   Maryland
olorado   **9**   Virginia   Washington, D.C.
Kansas   Missouri   **10**   Kentucky   (U.S. capital)
North Carolina
Tennessee
6   South Carolina
w   **8**   Oklahoma   Arkansas
exico   Alabama   **3**
12   Georgia
Texas   **11**
Louisiana   Florida
Mississippi

Compass Rose
North
West ◄●► East
South

Which Is Wackier?

Bubblegum Alley, San Luis Obispo, California

- These walls are covered in chewing gum. Do you think they are delightful...or disgusting?

- No one knows why sticking gum on the walls got started.

- The alley has been fully cleaned twice. But the cleanings never seem to stick! People just start covering the walls again.

You Decide!

Shoe Tree, Slab City, California

- Shoes do not usually grow on trees. But you will find many shoes on this one.

- People write their names or messages on their shoes before tossing them up.

- This isn't the only shoe tree in the United States. There are more!

Two Facts and a Fib

Woof! The World's Largest Beagle dog is doggone great! Its name is Sweet Willy. Its smaller pal is named Toby. Read the statements about them below. Two of them are true. Can you guess which one is false?

1. This is a good place to stop if you are tired on the road. You can spend the night inside Sweet Willy's belly.

2. The big red fire hydrant is a bathroom for people to use.

3. If you want to visit, leave your pup at home. Real dogs are not allowed.

Statement 3 is false. This is the Dog Bark Park Inn. Both people and their dogs are welcome to stay there.

Sweet Willy is in Cottonwood, Idaho.

Glossary

- **easels** (EE-zuhlz): folding stands with a small shelf that can hold something up, such as a painting

- **National Historic Landmark** (NA-shuh-nul hih-STOR-ik LAND-mark): building or place that is chosen for its importance in our country's history

- **sculpture** (SKULP-chur): piece of art, usually made of wood, stone, plaster, or metal

- **water towers** (WAH-tur TOW-erz): tall towers for storing water that goes through pipes into nearby homes and buildings

Index

Facts for Now

Visit this Scholastic Web site for more information on Roadside Attractions:

www.factsfornow.scholastic.com

Enter the keywords Roadside Attractions

About the Author

Pamela Chanko lives with her dog in New York City, where most people walk rather than drive. But after writing this book, a road trip may be in her future!